THE AMAZING LOST MAN

THE AMAZING LOST MAN

BEN PARKER

 **EYEWEAR** PUBLISHING

First published in 2016
by Eyewear Publishing Ltd
Suite 333, 19-21 Crawford Street
Marylebone, London W1H 1PJ
United Kingdom

Cover design and typeset by Edwin Smet
Cover photograph by Kirk Morgan
Author photograph by David Jones
Printed in England by TJ International Ltd, Padstow, Cornwall

ISBN 978-1-911335-39-9

*Eyewear wishes to thank Jonathan Wonham for his
generous patronage of our press.*

WWW.EYEWEARPUBLISHING.COM

For Katherine,
my perfect reader

Ben Parker's debut pamphlet,
The Escape Artists, was published by tall-
lighthouse in 2012 and shortlisted for the
2013 Michael Marks Award. He spent a year
as Poet-in-Residence at The Museum of
Royal Worcester, and in 2016 was
Poet-in-Residence at The Swan Theatre,
Worcester. He is poetry editor of
Critical Survey.

TABLE OF CONTENTS

THINGS ARE GROWING INSIDE HIS HOUSE

Mould in a petri dish, herbs lined
along the windowsill and flowerpots
making the dinner table unusable.
The indoor-ivy he planted last year
is preventing him reading authors
whose names position them on
the left side of his bookshelf. Does
dust grow or gather? He suspects
the latter but is hoping to justify
the former. A large topiary bush
in the shape of a topiary bush is
technically outside, but the kitchen
window is becoming increasingly
difficult to close. In the bathroom
there is little of either now, filled
instead with bonsai trees starting
to belie their name. During summer
he dare not sit in the lounge for fear
of crushing one of the visiting bees.
He does not grow lonely or old
before his time. Orchids are simpler
than people and more beautiful.
His youthful face is full of their light.

BRIDGEWATER TREATISE

If Babbage was correct,
that the residual motion of our speech
never truly fades
and all of human language
can be recovered

from a jar of air taken at random
from any piece of sky,
then might a single hawthorn twig
be sufficient
to trace the origin

of every other tree?
Their history written in a twist of cells,
strung like thin ribbon
along the dense flesh
packed within the heartwood.

Or take this glass of water
and let it stand for all those shores
we've never seen:
the burnt sand giving shape
to the ocean it contains,

the liquid moved from edge
to edge, not by the moon
but by your hand, tipping it first one way
then the other, to flash
beneath that lamp's small star.

SIDESHOW

The circus itches. Pipes play on
though there is no-one around to hear them.
The bones of candyfloss point the way
past the halted carousel and empty mirrors.
My appointment was two hours ago
if the fortune cookie is to be believed
but without knowing which of my services
is required it is hard to choose
from among the shrouded cages.
Licked sticks proliferate and I tread
the same giant discarded cartoon dog
deeper into mud. The tents are talking to me.
The strong-man sleeps in a fug of beer,
the dwarfs dream of Hollywood,
and I will still be here when dawn breaks.
Gather round! Watch as he checks a map
he doesn't have, see him turn on the spot
in the same exact place night after night,
and from this tower, madam, marvel
as he spells his own name eight-feet high
with his footprints, The Amazing Lost Man!

YIELD

These hard fruit
will hang unpicked
until their softer kin
are long consumed
or rotted on the vine:

gloss-skinned fists
bitter sun-refusers
they will not ripen
till the autumn moon
outshines the waning sun.

Tasted once, you give
their tree wide berth,
the bitter tang of flesh
lingering long after
you spat the first bite.

But something soon
presents to you again
those dark slung globes
and for no reason
that you can discern

a second taste is all
it takes for you to sit
beneath that canopy
of heavy leaves and live
devoted to their growth.

FROM THE HISTORIES

The Shogun's palace is surrounded
by a field of bells that always ring,
strung as they are on light ankle-high
wooden frames, designed to catch
the famous breeze lifting from the valley
and fanning constantly the open
courtyards and surrounding landscape
of this magnificent ancient dwelling.
So familiar is the movement of the air
to the Shogun, so deeply lodged
in the bloodline its seasonal changes
and daily agitations, that the orchestrated
music is as predictable to him
as his own heartbeat, and any disturbance
could indicate the advance of assassins
who, well-trained though they are
in the art of silent approach, cannot hear
an individual bell ring out of time
above the din. Even in drunken sleep
the Shogun knows when the tune is wrong
and wakes to dispatch his guards.
Thus his reign continues, and his family
will glorify the earth with their presence
for a thousand years, while their wives
and daughters stuff their ears with wax
and develop the intricate sign-language
for which their line is justly remembered.

A LECTURE ON THE [DIS]SIMILARITY
OF ORGANIC/INORGANIC OBJECTS

Is it true that there are no more trees,
or is it that I have forgotten
what they look like?

There are structures, I grant,
inclining more to the vertical
than the horizontal, which I recall was always

the case with trees,
but are these not rather people,
some of them, and lampposts others?

Or is it that there are
no more lampposts,
no more people, and only trees?

For trees I remember come in many shapes
and may well encompass
such arrangements as men, women,

postboxes and parking meters.
Furthermore
biologists and botanists have not

successfully restricted trees
to one or other unshared classification
to the exclusion of such

related but obviously distinct phenomena
as bushes, cacti, shrubs,
and other fauna.

Can we not expand from this
and say that rather than there being
no more streetlights,

no more people, that these in fact
have simply been subsumed
by that larger taxonomic family 'tree',

and I, untrained and inexperienced,
am unable to tell them
any more apart than I can tell

the difference between certain tall
specimens of grass
and a profusive, not yet budded, flower?

LEHNWORT

In this country where dawn is always just about to break
and snow sits like a migraine over everything, there are
creatures that move through the forest in the speech
of travellers. Their local name, the way it sounds like
the word for warmth, if warmth was a tool a warrior
might heft in battle, confines them to that part of the vast
language-spanning density of spruce and fir where they
were first spoken into being. But when a merchant risking
a short-cut on a trading route encounters their name
in gossip round the fire and trying to repeat it his tongue
falters on the unfamiliar vowels, then an echo of his hearth
creeps in, of his family's term for knife or the smell of damp
clinging to timber at the end of autumn. At this the creatures
stir from their sleep and begin the journey into fresh territory
while behind them thin trunks creak as frost tightens its grip.

CASTING THE EAGLE

For a while its every hatching
was half-formed and strange,
flat-winged albatross or hunched vulture:
we couldn't get the wing-span right

or fix the golden majesty we saw
in nature and even when we did
more often than not the kiln-heat
would crack the glory of it

as though the model caved
beneath the weight of too much beauty.
Frustrated, we cast aside the white shell
of its own unpainted plumage.

It took us more than a month
to re-conceive its delicate birth,
but today the first of its species
came out as we had always hoped:

furnace-born and freshly painted,
the whole so well done that tomorrow
we will hear of stunned crows fallen
below the window where it dries.

INSOMNIA POSTCARDS

Carnival on the main street

After the excitement of yesterday a welcome break.
Never before nor since. And the famous delicacy,
two fish kept together in a tank; when the larger
eats the smaller they are roasted immediately,
ungutted and whole. That was when he told me
that it does not pay to overexamine the simple things.
The young do not seem to offer the threat of violence,
but they are far from polite. The women work alone.
Green noon of overhanging leaves and the smoky
residue of many grills. Here at least is something.

Gentlemen at leisure

We arrived sometime later than planned. The cows
produce a milk that is the colour of sky awaiting sun
and there is a distinctive form of folk music that is
part elegy, part advertising jingle. Saffron, turmeric,
sandalwood, and many more. The sheen of freshly
polished steel. A man alone, eating raw seafood.
If I thought it would help, I would describe to you
the temperature. The cinema is closed for summer
though an organ still plays, like a solitary child.
They are taking down the ribbons from the trees.

Dawn over the mountains

Terrible architecture, but the footwear is marvellous.
Here truly is the promised land. When taking a swim
off the shore of a secluded beach this afternoon I came
to believe that 'ocean' is the default mode of this planet,
like a screensaver of almost infinitely complex scattered
particles. More slogans are invented daily, often
contradictory. Yes, I have had some encounters I do not
understand. The chemist I was sent to was stocked
mainly with overpriced coloured liquids. Red leaves
lifted by the wind are the only reason the red leaves fall.

Imperial statues

Birds fill the air with the percussion of flight, wheat
covers the hillsides like the fur of a large and docile
beast, at watch over the town. I can recommend
the local wine, the grapes are watered with the best
of last year's crop. A cairn of pebbles rubbed translucent
by children's hands. Helicopters patrol daily and clocks
chime at four minutes before the hour for reasons
of commerce. There is enough to be getting on with.
A small amount may be applied to the infected area
by a lover while you sleep if the pain continues.

Evening games

Knots of heavy foliage canopy the alleyways in which
small lizards dwell. Flags are kept at half-mast because
it is better to depress the living than disrespect the dead.
All day the slow manoeuvring of loaded trade ships.
The currency was recently discontinued as a result of
political turmoil. Present this note on your arrival and you
will be granted entry. No child is taught an instrument
until they have demonstrated the ability to manufacture
one of their own. Overhead wires hum softly; it is easy
to lose yourself in the leafy suburbs, beneath this sky.

ENDINGS

Allotments. Shattered chimney stacks.
A black bag tangled like a crow
in the leafless tree. As you walk

beyond the last of the deserted
red-brick factory buildings
the city rusts around you. The river

thins to a stream that could be forded
by a fallen branch. This is a place
of past tenses, an archaeology

of skeletal bikes, single gloves
and bleached cans of beer
the supermarkets no longer stock.

Spent matches hint at flame on flesh.
The rituals of childhood. Something
small and broken in the grass.

THE RESTAURANT

I
Most of the walls are black with the juice
of berries imported for just that purpose.
On those not daubed with the dark liquid
hang candid photos of your distant relatives
committing petty and archaic crimes.

II
The waiters are dressed for a funeral
and the concierge questions your levity
in the face of such grief. You are handed
a wine-list bound with the hair of every
beautiful woman who has ever dined there.

III
On entering, the lights are turned so high
you can feel the heat falling from them.
Within minutes the smell of sweating cheese
and humid fish has filled the dining area.
The windows and doors are sealed for effect.

IV
In place of menus are books of ingredients
subdivided into three independent segments,
such as are used by children to construct
chimeras. Someone has substituted one panel
of the main courses with one from the desserts.

V

The entire restaurant, including kitchen,
has been moved into the toilets while
'renovations' take place. On entering,
all parties are segregated by sex.
You may help yourself to the tap-water.

VI

A week before dining you must submit portraits
and brief summaries of friends with whom
you have lost touch. When you arrive the cooks
are wearing masks depicting your friends' faces
and mimic their mannerisms with absurd exaggeration.

VII

Sensitive microphones have been fixed
under some of the tables and the sounds
are relayed instantly to speakers set at a volume
just high enough to be heard. Today the first hints
of feedback are creeping into the layered chatter.

GHOSTS

When the ghosts of that house returned they came
not as ethereal figures looming in doorways, peering
over guests' shoulders in the bathroom mirror, or
ascending the stairs as the family arrived home late
just in time to catch sight of the bare feet. Instead
a chipped and frail porcelain cup suddenly appeared
in the cupboard above the sink and though no-one
would drink from it they could not bring themselves
to throw it away. Next, a thick string-bound volume
of correspondence was discovered on the bookshelf,
detailing the lives of characters at once familiar
but unplaceable, like distant cousins met at funerals.
Finally a pair of brogues was found by the back door,
so old that the only thing holding them together
was a deep layer of brown polish, freshly applied
with the singular dedication of someone for whom
these shoes were an unrepeatable extravagance.

REMEMBRANCES

for K.J.

A silver ring by the kitchen sink, your dress
embracing my jacket on the rail,
and on the floor those intimate blacks and reds
like crumpled flowers, lying where they fell.

By these tokens, and others, you let me know
forgetful as you are, you will return.
No sooner has the door clicked to
than I begin my search from room to room.

PAINTING YOUR VOICE

Not the actual words, you understand,
merely the shape your breath makes
when speaking, the way your tongue
works as a chisel on your sentences.

Perhaps the paint they use on gates,
the type that never dries, would work.
If I could stand at your side while you talk
in a room where the air is perfectly still.

Watch. Like smoke caught in a breeze
a contrail leads from the paintbrush
loaded at your lips to the whitewashed
opposite wall and leaves its mark.

Now let's step outside and find a hill
where the wind blows fiercely west
and let it take your speech and send it
like papers flung towards the sea.

Your voice is blossom on the ocean
carried by the tides to other shores,
other listeners. The heat will lift it up
and over mountains it will fall as rain.

THE KEY

When he died and we finally summoned the courage
to open the locked drawer in his office, we needed
first to force it, his set of keys having also disappeared
as if buried in the box with his body dressed for work.

Once inside we did not discover the pornographic stash
we'd feared, the illicit letters of our salacious guesses,
the half-finished bottle of our noirish ones. Instead
it was simply this: the key to the lock we had prised

and no doubt broken in the process. There was no
mistaking it, all of us had seen it quickly turned
each time we entered unannounced this room
of his retreat. Had he known he was going to die

and hidden the contents elsewhere, or burned them,
leaving a copy of this key as reprimand? Or was
this drawer, sealing in its snug coffin the means
to its own release, his final message? Had all those

sudden furtive lockings been a ruse to bring us here?
To show perhaps that certain secrets are secret only
for the sake of holding something back. That if we keep
nothing else from those we love we should keep that.

ONE PLACE

Out here the elms echo with the eagle-shout
and sparrow-cry; leaves tune the wind;
the only path is the one your trespass cuts.

Your car is waiting at the forest's edge
with autumn already falling on its roof.
You bag and bury your mud clad-shoes

before rejoining the nightly homeward grind,
just another commuter locked to a private frequency.
Delay can be explained by deadlines,

accidents or (at a push) affairs. Your wife
would sooner sanction a sexual betrayal
than bless your return here,

the one place still forbidden to you both.

FORECAST

When you are primed for cold
by the chill contained
in German Bight and Irish Sea
the name of Iceland washes up
the image of a lone boat,
its signal-light the only star
in a tiny universe of fog.
For the few occupants
of that squall-rocked vessel
the radio's words are more
than just a childhood riddle:
out there in the salt-dark
it is the only reminder
that they are not forgotten.
The rain is easing. Moderate
or poor is becoming good.

THE PATH

Near my old ancestral home is a village
at whose tree-lined edge

a path begins
which doesn't end

until it reaches the corner
of the horn of Africa

and dries up on a beach.
Its reach

requires that it twice slide into the ocean
with no more concern

than when a car dips
into a valley filled with mist

emerging with its lights still lit
the bonnet wet

and the passengers none the wiser
at the next rise.

It is only as wide
as two horses side by side

and thin
from many months of walking.

THE ROCK WATCHERS

Outside the spring is under way,
that centre-stage fluent trajectory
of coloured backdrop
and curtain raised. It fills windows
everywhere and most particularly

the one behind which I stand
to observe the final claim
of winter on the land: the stone
that holds within its mineral shell
the remnant cold collected

from the last snow that fell
before warmth returned and forced
the chill to take its refuge like a bird
in hibernation, weathering
not the frost but the thaw that follows.

As occupant of this overlooking room
I have the task of keeping safe
this storehouse of a season
and am forbidden to either touch
or let it leave my sight.

If my attendance is successful
come autumn a spark will still remain
from which the ice might grow
and in its turn compel the vagrant heat
to find a secret dwelling of its own.

HOUSE OF RIVERS

For days you hear the din of wind
through trees as simply that, until
your fire hangs a cord of smoke
from the sky, straight as a plumb-line,
and your finger comes down damp

with the lick you planted on it still warm
and you know that you are close. Two hours
and you are facing the house. By now
the sound has grown so loud
it seems that all the rivers of the world

have burst their banks to run as one.
The walls are unscrolling from the roof
and going to ground in broken waves;
the door stands open centre left,
as though a rock or fallen branch

has blocked the water's path.
The Earth tips back to point at dusk
and sun shines clear through the frame
lighting the unobstructed stream
bending unbidden round the lintel.

You step inside and in an hour your skin
is bloated, after two you no longer
blink at the spray coughed in your face.
By morning your lungs have shrunk
to stones, your neck flares as you breathe.

RETICULATED VASE

as he shapes the wet clay
with absolute clarity of purpose
he must feel like some minor deity

revealing the delicate and exquisite
creature of his dreams
finding in damp earth a fragile heart

that grows more extravagant
the more he cuts away
until absence defines a silhouette

which stands revealed as space
suspended by more space
bird bone   white hive   ghost vase

THE CINEMA IN THE WOODS

In the woods behind your house
            there is a cinema
that is so old the screen
                        is stripped bark
and the seats are oak stumps.

There is no organ accompaniment
only the mournful call
of a solitary owl.

The acorns are nourishing but bland.

Each evening the phosphorescent glow
                of the latest feature
            brings an audience of moths
who do not appreciate the extensive use
of dream sequence.

I think about you and how much you
            would appreciate the extensive
                        use of dream sequence.

All of the films shown here concern you

            and most particularly your hair
                        and its appearance
in different qualities of light/weather.

Tonight there is a slight breeze. Your hair
                is lit by a neon sign.
It is a paradise of amber wings.

UNTITLED

The empty plot behind our flat
is a place of mushrooms, damp
discarded wood, rusted tools

and uncertain ownership.
Autumn will return it to itself,
to that rain you can hear

but barely feel, the static blur
of a radio lost between stations
freed from the discipline of signal.

INSOMNIA POSTCARDS

War memorial

Dark sea suggestive of depth. Sharp rocks revealed
by the waning tide. A lone cormorant scuds across.
There is a kind of sweet dough laced with butterscotch
and served warm, which is widely available. No one
is able to direct me to the border. All the street lights
are tinted to indicate the primary function of each area:
blue for retail, green for residential, red for construction.
Blankets are woven to mark every birth and the size
usually corresponds to the wealth of the family. When
the season ends all the menus are revised accordingly.

A sunset vista

I think that the blues here are more blue than
those anywhere else. Highly varnished pine gates
open to semi-covered workshops where the old
repair the guns used by the young in the endless
war. All buildings are angled approximately 1° west.
Underwater aqueducts are available for irrigation
and also transport. We wake at 6 most days. It is
the vast dream of our being together, the vagueness
of outer-space. There are systems of control. Don't
ask me about the details, I am not qualified to expand.

View from the hotel

Most of the doors open on to further doors, which
open on to courtyards, inevitably. Peeling the wrapping
from a cigarette packet is a wordless benediction. Under
your bare feet the sand is dark as damp linen, let me
dip my toes in one more time, for the pleasure of it.
It is enough that these things salute us: cured meats,
stray animals, a quarrel of car horns, warm bread served
at breakfast. There are optical illusions about which
your first thought was the correct one, others that you
will never resolve. Waves come in like adoring crowds.

Outside the palace

The way these shadows are cast is magnificent,
but I am unable to explain the difference between
polished silver and a mirror. Something changes.
At dusk, love's ample disarrangement. The band
is playing old-style tunes, though the occasional
contemporary number is included in order to placate
the management. I've heard that it takes more than
two decades to master the local dialect, by which time
most of the words are obsolete anyway. A magician
sits down to smoke. Dust is lifted by passing cars.

Waterfront

Huge steel gantries stretch in every direction, office
blocks are lost in cloud, the cloud is lost in smoke.
Not all lengths have easily assignable numeric terms.
Two owls audition for the zodiac. The military gathers
at noon every week day and there is an artist who insists
on painting each side of his large canvases just in case.
Brochures detailing the most beautiful local attractions
are long out of date but still widely available. Whatever
you do, don't let me forget to show you the market,
its many wonders. So much is easily paraphrasable.

ORNITHOLOGY

There is a type of bird whose mating call comes
not from its throat but the inside of its egg.
So, while the female's shell lodges the lives
of feathered embryos, the male's encloses air.

When it is laid the casing dries and shrinks
and the carefully uneven surface starts to crack,
releasing the first note as a signal, its pitch levelled
perfectly to reach the ears of the intended mate.

Then each fault-line breaks in sequence and the slow
unstitching gifts its song. About a minute in
enough pressure is still contained to sound
a harmony of chords, which either achieve their aim

or break the casing and the bird must wait
another year to pair. And with so much depending
on success, some island variants lay their eggs
near mountain peaks or cliffs to catch the April winds.

At high-points such as these it has been known
for females to keep a vigil lasting weeks, and if
the weather holds its course the rocks in June
are still obscured by hunched attentive listeners.

Do you remember that day we found the first horse?
It was skittering the dust in a forgotten field adjacent to
a farmhouse that must have stood forever if not longer.
This was the horse from which all other horses were
bred; the horse of cave-paintings and untranslatable
mythology. Undomesticated, rough-haired, and small,
it looked more like a mongrel dog. We took it to the
backyard of our rented ground-floor flat. Our friends
came over to see it. That's a dog, they told us. We
resolved not to speak to them again. We brought our
horse fresh-cut grass every spring and oats throughout
the winter but it grew thin and restless. We asked your
uncle, the vet, to inspect it for us. He took you into a
corner and spoke in a gentle concerned tone, as though
he had forgotten you were an adult. You sent him away
and cried for a bit. That evening, to cheer you up, we
watched a documentary on horses and thought how
proud our horse must be to have delivered this noble
race. Do you remember the day we found the first horse
chewing a rubber ball thrown over by the neighbours?

THE MEETING

In this latitude, winter mornings
have a washed-clean effect
as though in preparation
for the sweat and dust of the year ahead.

Just so is today's cloudless blue.

It will be in conditions such as these,
with mist still in the valley
and the condensation not yet evaporated
from the windows,
that I shall dress in my smartest suit
and head out to meet him.

I will descend three flights of stairs
and make the short walk to the café
where I'll drink a breakfast vodka
and watch the smoke of a dozen cigarettes.

He will already have been there
for longer than I can imagine and when I leave
there he will remain,
casual as the echo of a gunshot.

POEM BEGINNING WITH A QUOTE FROM ALAN GARNER

The first time I was declared dead I was two.
The second time I was declared dead I'd recovered before
    the thrown ball hit the grass.
The third time I was declared dead, our family dog stopped
    eating and stared mournfully at my limp body.
The fourth time, the lifted glass trembled briefly but the
    wine was not spilled.
The fifth time I was declared dead no one noticed and I had
    to make the announcement myself.
The sixth time, paramedics were on hand within a matter
    of seconds but were disappointed to discover that
    the crisis had already passed and I was reviving
    myself with minimal difficulty.
The seventh time was a mistake.
The eighth time I was declared dead was a dawn of glorious
    sunlight and I wept to be confined in blackness even
    momentarily and from that day forth I have gone in
    fear of night.
When I was declared dead by a woman I had hoped to seduce
    it was only one of many refusals and I did not take it
    unduly to heart.
The tenth time I was declared dead was mortifying and I will
    not speak of it.
The eleventh time I was declared dead I was glad of the rest,
    having slept poorly all that week.

The twelfth time, the heavy news was delivered by courier
    but I was unable to answer the door and found only
    a note informing me I'd been out.

The thirteenth time I was declared dead was no
      unluckier than the others and confirmed my
      belief that superstition is mere delusion.
The fourteenth time came as a surprise.
The fifteenth through twenty-ninth times I was declared
      dead were not particularly remarkable and
      somewhere around the thirties I lost count.
I am hoping that on the one hundredth occasion I will
      receive a telegram from whoever is monarch at
      that point, so that I may resume my accurate
      record.

THE SOUNDING BOWL

Out of the log that he salvaged from the wind-felled
walnut tree the carpenter removed so much wood
that what remained behind was closer in spirit to air
than to earth, that element first hinted by its fall
and perfected by the careful hand of man, who dug
the bole to find the bowl and varnished the grain until
it gave no more resistance to the breeze gusting through
his workshop than the ear would to a whispered
prayer. Those strings he fitted across the open mouth
were nothing more than cues to wake the latent music,
so easily set off it was as though the song had been there
long before the storm released it. The carpenter, his part
complete, is content now to give the instrument
to the world, knowing that no matter who it is that plays,
all sounding bowls sing hymns to the glory of their makers.

ALTERED LIFE

Sleepless still at dawn you leave the house
to go where you can watch
rust spreading over exposed metal

like ink across cotton, the place
of bark visibly tightening around oak
and light that falls as slow as cooling pitch,

knowing that each afternoon
you will wake to hear yolk smother the white
in an empty kitchen.

In the eyes of strangers now
there is the shadow of an altered life
in which you were taken

to a country of pungent nameless meats,
music played on the bones of children
and markets that last for weeks;

where the sun is a glare on stone buildings
and priests bend their grey heads
to pray for the health of youthful gods.

3A

You called me to the living room to hear
a strangled outburst coming from beyond
our glass and mortar guard against such things
but I arrived too late and got instead
the echo you produced which left us both
in shock that such a cry might issue from
a human throat.
                          Yet having learned it could
we wondered if it had and though I tried
to reassure with talk of owls and crows
and though you tried to take your utterance back
we listen to the darkness now aware
it once contained that sound and may again.

INSOMNIA POSTCARDS

Skyline at night

All encyclopaedias here are totally blank. The church
has acknowledged this fact. The cares of the many
are sharp branches in the woods we journey through.
Twelve different types of water are available in most
shops and even the basic hotel rooms have five taps.
Hot and cold are just the start of it. Do not give money
to the beggars for they are the government funded
representatives of an authenticity campaign. Thunder
reiterated by intricate valleys. No, and I will probably
not get the chance. Excellent service, thank you again.

Inside the museum

The only card games well known are for one player
or less. Beneath the barrow, bones stir. What isn't
bolted down is hung up. Things drift across. As far
as I can tell this is non-negotiable. Everything here
costs the same, but heavier items are no doubt harder
to transport and dedicated couriers are provided for
exactly this reason. I am unable to describe to you
the monuments, I simply do not possess the necessary
words. Ritual is observed. Sediment builds. I mostly
just watch television. Elm grows pretty indiscriminately.

Ships at port

We travelled mainly for financial reasons, words
spoken like the pieces of a difficult puzzle, a red book
open on a chair. The foliage is exclusively confined
to windowboxes. Something is concealed. A darkness
so deep, torches merely serve to draw attention to it.
Passing along the beach front today I was accosted
by a merchant, who claimed to have known my father,
having fought alongside him in the war. Dinner is almost
served and I have been lied to. Your details are already
printed on the left and the sky spreads out below you.

A crowded café

In the strong wind large trees bend like subjects
bowing before the emperor. We have been so long
together now that I can no longer smell your hair
as you step dripping from the shower. After music
business as usual, the clatter of passing food carts
and trinket sellers. Without going into detail, the day
was 'satisfactory'. Walking back from the temple
after a particularly instructive sermon it is possible
to notice such things as the laughter of soldiers,
the intricate lattice-work on baskets, this gold coin.

Various scenes

The city is lit by a series of large curved mirrors
directing the sun's light into the deep valley. Gongs
and the passing of migratory birds. We were given
small bags holding clay figures representing heroes
of the national mythology. The rains held off though
for much of the week clouds gathered in the east
like a clandestine senate discussing revolution.
Zip-lock containers of sweet berries are provided
for consumption on significant days. A dog will pass
in the street sometimes. It will be the same dog.

A REQUEST

If I die before you, do not forget
the promise that you made me:
that you will somehow find a way
to slip this speaker in the coffin
before I burn or am buried.
It is not primed to play a calming
piece of music to soothe me
should the dead feel fear, nor
does the microchip contain
words of comfort for those
still living, that if an afterlife
exists I'll see them there. No,
this is that recording we planned
all those years ago: me, banging
on a wooden box and asking
sternly to be let out now please.

THE RADIO'S WORDS

It was about then that he began
tuning in to the shipping forecast
as it drifted across near-empty seas
three times a day, to an audience
that he supposed must be dwindling
by the week, air-freight and fisheries
diminishing the once-ubiquitous
importance of the ocean. Was it
this that drew him to those strange
numerals, the melancholy locations
isolated at the edge of our island?
It certainly wasn't for information.
It is true that it soothed him, but even
after the midnight broadcast ended
he would not sleep, and instead
he liked to think that those few
left out there on the water still awake
were imagining him, a man at home:
warm, stationary, and for no reason
he or they would fathom, inclining
his head for the list he knew by heart
and the conditions he never guessed.

SUBJECT

We can hear her bird heart beating its life
deep in the cage of her chest. It is so loud
we suspect that it is trying to break free.

We give her stones to lay on the feathers
so the heart will remain where it belongs
but still it strains against her fragile breast.

We fit a small net across her open mouth
and keep a constant watch in case the bird
flies from its perch and rises to the light.

We are ready to clip its wings if we must.
We have stopped providing the dry seed
and every day now it grows a little calmer.

FORM

You all know the trick:
shape your searching hand
into a crude approximation
of the lost object, so that
summoned by its form
made flesh the scissors,
tennis ball, or plastic lighter
will appear. A simple act
of sympathetic magic.
But have you considered
expanding on this law
and shaping not just
the singular and small
but calling forth instead
larger, complex entities?
What configuration
of fingers would represent
a house? A fleet of cars?
And why stop at the concrete
if you could figure out
the symbol for respect,
or adoration. The elaborate
interlocking of thumbs
and knuckles that stands
for luck or fortune. The way
to hold your hands for love.

CHURCH FLATTS FARM

All night the waves are in his room
lifting him from half-dreams
of bladder-wrack and drift-wood.
The walls breathe like filling sails,
the blood-tide beats in his ears,
he is feverish and sleepless, far
from instruments, with no navigator
and the Pole Star lost behind plaster.

When arthritis closed around his hands
he left the sea and made his way here,
the furthest he could move inland,
and stripped his boat to make a bed.
Mornings now he wakes with dry lips,
salt-blur glazing the window.

WORKING THE KILN

Thick air. Dry brick-dust. Fumes.
Swaddled in damp cloth
we enter again that dragon-cave

to return as steaming thieves
clutching the delicate egg
of porcelain, taking it to that cool

the kilns we work in never know
and dousing ourselves deep
in the horse-trough to gain relief.

Each morning we cook our bacon
in seconds, plunge our hands
in ice to keep the blisters back.

20.10.15

That was the warm autumn
when the flies appeared.
Two weeks of cold
and we thought we'd seen
the last of them.
But summer has returned
in mid-October
bringing with it
that dark congregation
who occupy the roof:
the sun is their minister
and these hot slates
his pews that must be filled.
Like any flock
they soon grow curious
about the space below
and through the sky-light vents
they come,
dozens gathered
on the wrong side
of the glass.
They are tired, and regretting
their descent agitate
at the edges, trying
to find escape.
A swung towel would be enough
to bring them down.
But they look so single-minded
in their need,
not like the wild black pellets
of June who throw themselves

directionless
at every surface,
that I fling the velux wide
and watch them slant the blue.
Within the hour
they will be back
and again I will be required
to set them free.

ADMITTING NO OTHER ELEMENT

Deep in the feathers of certain birds
nestle microscopic versions of that bird
beating their wings in unison for flight,
and lifting not as a flock, but as one;

then there are those large cats in Africa
on whose teeth crouch smaller
and smaller identical cats, right down
to a level we cannot yet observe;

and I once ate a strawberry
in which every seed was a tiny
strawberry, and it was the most
delicious strawberry that I ever tasted.

I watch your face as you listen to me
explaining this, and you are a thousand
yous, each one alike, and the more
I look at them the more of you I see.

THE WAY

Drive again through the last outlying
rain-shuttered village, beyond
the final fuel stop, past where the road inclines,
inclines again, then levels out.
Tune the radio to the dead melodies
of that country's only great composer
and focus on the dwindling road ahead.
As you move outside the station's reach
wait for the rising background static
to mingle with the trumpet's sombre tone
and when the closing note
is lost beneath that black scrawl
crank the volume dial clockwise
drop your windows, let your car become
a needle in a groove of infinite diameter.
That sound is not the shifting of the continents,
not the heaving of the gathered clouds
or stretching of the oak's dark roots.
That sound is not your lover's breath
but tonight it's near enough.

HOW SHE REMEMBERS

On the rare occasions
when she walks in woodland alone
the muffled blows
of a distant woodpecker
bring back no memories
of her grandmother, pausing
mid-step, head cocked
and thin arm raised like a bare branch,
signalling the sound of her favourite bird;

nor does the smell
of freshly brewed Costa Rican coffee
remind her of her father
back from his year-long 'indiscretion'
in a mountain village,
tamping the grounds like gunpowder
and making her try just one more time
that drink for which
she never developed a taste.

But if she steps outside
slightly underdressed for the year's
first crop of snow
she is back at her mother's house
and the frozen week she spent
rising an hour early
and lifting the lid of ice
from all the neighbours' ponds
to allow the fish to breathe;

and at the height of summer
when the office air conditioning failed
she stared at her cubicle wall
and saw the beach
where she lost an afternoon
burying all the watches she could steal
so everyone might remain
where they were, lying
in that heat forever.

ACKNOWLEDGMENTS

My thanks to the editors of the following magazines, where some of these poems were first published: *Agenda, Body, Confingo, Elbow Room, Fake Poems, The Harlequin, Hinterland, The Journal, Neon, Orbis, The Poetry Shed, Popshot, Shadowtrain, Under the Radar, Veild the Pole,* and *The White Review.*

Some of these poems appeared in *The Escape Artists* (2012) published by tall-lighthouse and *From the Porcelain* (2015) published by The Museum of Royal Worcester.

Thank you to everyone who has given feedback and advice on these poems.

 **EYEWEAR** PUBLISHING